From Purchase to
Profit: A
Beginner's Guide
to Selling Online
Courses

Janika Hall

FROM PURCHASE TO PROFIT

A Beginner's Guide to Selling Online Courses

By
Janika Hall

Table of Contents

Note from the Author

Dear Reader,

Thank you for purchasing "From Purchase to Profit: A Beginner's Guide to Selling Online Courses." It's truly an honor to have you embark on this journey with us.

Before diving into the wealth of information contained within these pages, I want to express my heartfelt gratitude for your trust and confidence in this guide. Whether you're a seasoned entrepreneur or just starting your online course business, I believe you'll find valuable insights and strategies to help you succeed in the dynamic world of online education.

I want to emphasize that while this guide provides practical advice and proven strategies for generating passive income through selling online courses, it is not a get-rich-quick scheme. Building a successful online education business requires dedication, hard work, and a commitment to providing value to your audience.

Throughout this journey, remember that success is not measured by overnight riches, but by the impact you make and the value you create for your customers. Stay focused, stay resilient, and never underestimate the power of continuous learning and improvement.

Once again, thank you for choosing "From Purchase to Profit." I wish you all the best on your path to building a thriving online course business.

Warm regards,

Janika Hall

Author of "From Purchase to Profit: A Beginner's Guide to Selling Online Courses"

INTRODUCTION

Welcome to "From Purchase to Profit: A Beginner's Guide to Selling Online Courses," your essential roadmap to navigating the rewarding world of online education as a business. The digital age has brought about countless opportunities to learn and earn, and one of the most lucrative and fulfilling ways to participate is through selling online courses. Whether you are an expert looking to share your knowledge or an entrepreneur seeking new income streams, this guide will provide you with the tools and insights you need to succeed.

The Power of Online Courses

Online courses have revolutionized the way we think about education and professional development. With the internet bridging gaps between instructors and learners across the globe, anyone can access educational materials at any time, and from anywhere. This accessibility not only makes it easier for learners to enhance their skills but also opens up a vast market for course creators. By turning your knowledge into a structured online course, you not only contribute to this vibrant educational ecosystem but also establish a potential source of income that can grow and evolve with your expertise.

Understanding MRR and PLR

As you embark on your journey to create and sell online courses, you'll encounter various methods by which you can market and distribute your content. Two particularly interesting options are Master Resell Rights (MRR) and Private Label Rights (PLR) courses.

- Master Resell Rights (MRR) allow you to sell the course to customers along with the rights to resell it. This means that not only can your customers learn from the content, but they can also turn around and sell it to others, keeping 100% of the profits.

- Private Label Rights (PLR) goes a step further by allowing you to modify, rebrand, and claim the content as your own. This means you can tailor the content to better fit your brand or your audience's needs, potentially increasing its value and uniqueness in the marketplace.

Benefits of MRR and PLR for Passive Income

Using MRR and PLR courses can significantly enhance your ability to generate passive income. These rights allow you to leverage content created by others to build a portfolio of products without the time investment required to create courses from scratch. They offer a quick route to market expansion and can be an excellent way to diversify your income streams. With smart marketing and strategic positioning, MRR and PLR courses can continuously generate revenue with minimal ongoing effort.

This book is designed to guide you through every step of your online course selling journey—from understanding the basics of digital products to advanced strategies for maximizing your earnings. Let's dive in and explore how you can transform your knowledge and resources into profitable online courses!

Chapter 1: Understanding Resell Rights

In this opening chapter, we delve into the specifics of resell rights, focusing primarily on Master Resell Rights (MRR) and Private Label Rights (PLR). These are two powerful tools in the arsenal of digital product sales, allowing creators and marketers to maximize their earnings with relatively low ongoing effort.

- Master Resell Rights (MRR) provide you with the ability to sell not only the course itself but also the rights to resell it. This means your buyers can legally sell the course to others. MRR typically includes fewer restrictions on sales compared to other rights, offering a versatile option for rapid distribution and profit.

- Private Label Rights (PLR) allows you to modify, rebrand, and essentially claim the course as your own. You can alter the content, change its components, and sell it under your brand. This flexibility makes PLR especially valuable for creating a unique product that stands out in the market.

Comparison and Considerations

While both MRR and PLR can be lucrative, they serve different purposes and come with distinct legal considerations. Understanding the nuances between them is crucial for leveraging their potential while adhering to legal standards. MRR is typically more straightforward, focusing on resale without modification, whereas PLR offers more creative control but requires careful management to avoid brand dilution or market saturation.

Legal Implications and Limitations

Navigating the legal landscape of MRR and PLR is essential. This chapter will explore the common legal implications and limitations associated with these rights, ensuring you use them effectively and ethically. From copyright issues to licensing restrictions, knowing these details can protect you from potential pitfalls and help maintain the integrity of your business.

By the end of this chapter, you'll have a solid foundation in the types of resell rights available and how to use them strategically to benefit your online course business. Let's get started on transforming your knowledge into a profitable digital empire!

Ready to learn and earn? Turn the page, and let's begin our journey from purchase to profit.

Chapter 2: Advantages of Master Resell Rights Courses

Welcome to Chapter 2 of "From Purchase to Profit: A Beginner's Guide to Selling Online Courses." In this chapter, we'll explore the significant advantages of using Master Resell Rights (MRR) courses to build and expand your online educational business. MRR courses offer unique benefits that can streamline your entry into the market and enhance your profit potential.

Time and Cost Efficiency

One of the most compelling reasons to choose MRR courses is their time and cost efficiency. Creating a course from scratch involves substantial investment in time, effort, and money. You need to plan the curriculum, create the content, test the materials, and much more. However, with MRR courses, the heavy lifting has already been done. You purchase the rights to a course that has been fully developed, allowing you to bypass the creation process and jump straight to selling. This immediate time-saving can be a game-changer, especially for those new to the digital education scene or those looking to expand quickly without the corresponding overhead costs.

Profit Potential with Unlimited Selling

MRR courses come with the incredible advantage of allowing unlimited selling. Once you own the rights, you can sell the course to as many customers as you like, without any restrictions on the number of sales. This unlimited selling potential means that your initial investment in purchasing the rights could be recouped multiple times over, offering a high return on investment. The more you market and sell, the more you earn, turning a single purchase into a continuous income stream.

Immediate Access to Complete Course Materials

When you acquire MRR for a course, you gain immediate access to complete, market-ready course materials. This includes everything from the course content itself to supplementary materials that enhance the learning experience. Having a ready-to-market product not only speeds up your time to market but also reduces the stress and uncertainty of developing course materials yourself.

Overview of Typical Contents in MRR Courses

MRR courses are typically comprehensive and designed to provide a complete learning experience. Let's break down what you might typically find in these courses:

- Modules: MRR courses are often structured into modules, each covering different aspects of the subject. This modular approach helps in organizing the learning process and makes it easier for users to follow.

- Quizzes: To enhance engagement and retention, quizzes are frequently included to test the learner's understanding of the material covered. These are essential for educational courses as they provide both you and your users with feedback on the learning progress.

- Videos: Video content is a staple of modern online courses due to its effectiveness in engagement and information retention. MRR courses often include professionally made videos that explain complex topics in a digestible format.

- Additional Resources: Many MRR courses also come with extra resources like worksheets, eBooks, slideshows, and more. These materials support the learning experience and add value for the user, making the course more appealing.

By leveraging the benefits of MRR courses, you can efficiently and effectively enter the online education market with a quality product that has unlimited earning potential. With the groundwork laid and the path clear, you're ready to take your next steps toward making a mark in the world of online courses. Ready to move forward? Let's dive into how to effectively market these courses in the next chapter!

Welcome to Chapter 3 of "From Purchase to Profit: A Beginner's Guide to Selling Online Courses." In this chapter, we'll delve into the essential considerations for choosing the right Master Resell Rights (MRR) courses to maximize your success in the online education market. Selecting the right courses is crucial for attracting and retaining customers, so let's explore the key factors you need to keep in mind.

Factors to Consider When Selecting an MRR Course

Before diving into the world of MRR courses, it's essential to consider a few key factors that will guide your decision-making process:

- Relevance: Ensure that the course content aligns with your expertise and interests. Choose topics that you are knowledgeable about and passionate about sharing with others.

- Market Demand: Research the market demand for the course topic. Look for subjects that are trending or have a consistent demand over time. Analyze keywords, search volumes, and competitor offerings to gauge the potential interest in your chosen course.

- Quality: Assess the quality of the course materials, including the content, presentation, and supplementary resources. Look for well-researched content, engaging visuals, and clear explanations that will captivate your audience.

- Licensing Terms: Review the licensing terms carefully to ensure they align with your business goals and legal obligations. Understand any restrictions on editing, branding, or resale, and choose courses that offer flexibility and freedom within these parameters.

Understanding Your Target Audience's Needs

To effectively sell MRR courses, you must have a deep understanding of your target audience's needs, preferences, and pain points. Consider the following questions:

- Who is your ideal customer? Define the demographics, interests, and behaviors of your target audience.

- What are their goals and challenges? Identify the problems or aspirations that your audience is seeking solutions for.

- How can your course help them? Determine how your chosen MRR courses can address your audience's needs and provide value.

By aligning your course selection with your audience's interests and preferences, you increase the likelihood of attracting and retaining customers.

Evaluating Course Quality and Content Relevance

When evaluating MRR courses, it's essential to assess both the quality of the content and its relevance to your audience. Consider the following criteria:

- Content Depth: Evaluate the depth and breadth of the course content. Ensure that it covers the topic comprehensively and provides actionable insights and strategies.

- Engagement: Look for courses that engage learners through interactive elements, case studies, real-life examples, and practical exercises.

- Up-to-Date Information: Verify that the course content is current and reflects the latest industry trends, research findings, and best practices.

- User Reviews: Seek feedback from other users who have purchased and used the course. User reviews can provide valuable insights into the course quality and effectiveness.

By carefully considering these factors and aligning your course selection with your audience's needs, you can choose MRR courses that have the potential to drive sales and generate revenue in the competitive online education market.

With the right courses in your arsenal, you're well-equipped to embark on your journey to selling online courses and achieving success in the digital education landscape. In the next chapter, we'll explore effective strategies for marketing your MRR courses and reaching your target audience. Let's dive in!

Welcome to Chapter 4 of "From Purchase to Profit: A Beginner's Guide to Selling Online Courses." In this chapter, we'll explore the top 8 sources for Master Resell Rights (MRR) courses, each offering a unique selection of courses tailored to different niches and audiences. Let's dive into these valuable resources and discover how they can help you build your online course empire.

1. Content Sparks

Content Sparks specializes in courses focused on sales, marketing, business, and self-development topics. Their courses come with a detailed breakdown of what's included, such as course books, quizzes, sales pages, and more. While their offerings may be priced higher compared to other sources, they provide exceptional value and comprehensive materials to kickstart your online course business.

2. PLR.me

PLR.me is known for its self-improvement, relationships, and finance courses. They offer extensive customization options and content formats, including TXT, PDF, and WORD files. With their unique pricing structure and starter credits, PLR.me provides flexibility for those looking to create personalized courses tailored to their audience's needs.

3. Coach Glue

Designed specifically for coaches, Coach Glue emphasizes marketing and entrepreneurship topics. Their comprehensive packages include worksheets, checklists, and marketing materials, making it easy for coaches to create and sell high-quality courses. With transparent pricing and VIP pass options, Coach Glue offers a convenient solution for coaches looking to expand their offerings.

4. Tools For Motivation

Tools For Motivation specializes in self-help content, offering a range of courses to help individuals improve their wellbeing and personal development. They provide an overview of course contents and customization options, ensuring that users can create courses that resonate with their audience. With detailed pricing for courses and additional content, Tools For Motivation makes it simple to access high-quality resources for personal growth.

5. PLR Database

PLR Database offers membership-based access to a wide range of niches, including business, marketing, health, and more. They provide both Master Resell and Private Label offerings, allowing users to choose the licensing option that best suits their needs. With competitive membership pricing and benefits, PLR Database offers a cost-effective solution for accessing a diverse selection of courses and content.

6. Berkeley Wellbeing Institute

With a focus on wellbeing and personal development courses, Berkeley Wellbeing Institute offers courses designed to help individuals improve their mental and emotional health. They provide flexibility in content customization and offer transparent pricing for their courses, ensuring that users can create courses that align with their brand and audience.

7. Problemio

Problemio offers courses focused on business and marketing, created by a top Udemy instructor. They provide detailed licensing details and content customization options, allowing users to tailor courses to their specific needs. With transparent pricing tiers and lifetime updates, Problemio offers a reliable solution for accessing high-quality courses in the business and marketing niche.

8. PLR Products

PLR Products offers a general overview of available course types, including video courses and ebook packs, covering a wide range of topics. They provide search tips for navigating the platform and highlight their affordability and range of topics, making them a suitable option for those looking for budget-friendly course options.

With these top 8 sources for MRR courses, you have access to a wealth of resources to kickstart your online course business. Whether you're looking to specialize in a specific niche or offer a diverse range of courses, these sources offer the flexibility and variety you need to succeed.

Welcome to Chapter 5 of "From Purchase to Profit: A Beginner's Guide to Selling Online Courses." In this chapter, we'll explore strategies for effectively marketing and selling your Master Resell Rights (MRR) courses. While having high-quality courses is essential, successful selling requires strategic marketing efforts to reach your target audience and drive sales. Let's dive into some key strategies to help you promote your courses and maximize your earning potential.

Introduction to Digital Product Sales

Before diving into specific marketing strategies, it's essential to understand the concept of digital product sales and its benefits compared to physical products.

- Understanding Digital Products: Digital products are intangible goods that are delivered electronically, such as online courses, ebooks, software, and digital downloads. Unlike physical products, digital products can be easily distributed, accessed, and replicated, making them an attractive option for online entrepreneurs.

- Benefits of Selling Online Courses as Digital Products: Selling online courses as digital products offers several advantages, including:

- Low Overhead Costs: Digital products require minimal overhead costs for production, storage, and distribution, allowing you to maximize your profits.

- Instant Delivery: Digital products can be delivered instantly to customers via email or download links, providing immediate access to course materials.

- Scalability: Digital products can be easily scaled to accommodate a growing customer base without the need for additional resources or infrastructure.

Strategies for Effective Online Course Marketing

Marketing your MRR courses effectively is crucial for attracting potential buyers and driving sales. Here are some strategies to consider:

- Identify Your Target Audience: Understand who your ideal customers are and tailor your marketing efforts to appeal to their interests and needs.

- Create Compelling Content: Develop engaging content that highlights the value and benefits of your courses. Use persuasive language and visuals to capture the attention of your audience.

- Utilize Social Media: Leverage social media platforms to promote your courses and engage with your audience. Share valuable content, interact with followers, and use targeted advertising to reach potential buyers.

- Email Marketing: Build an email list of interested prospects and regularly send them valuable content, promotions, and updates about your courses. Email marketing can be a powerful tool for nurturing leads and driving sales.

SEO Tips for Course Sellers

Optimizing your course content for search engines can help improve your visibility and attract organic traffic to your website. Here are some SEO tips to consider:

- Keyword Research: Identify relevant keywords related to your courses and incorporate them strategically into your website content, including course titles, descriptions, and landing pages.

- Optimize Metadata: Write compelling meta titles and descriptions that accurately describe your courses and entice users to click through to your website.

- Create High-Quality Content: Produce valuable, informative content that addresses the needs and interests of your target audience. This can include blog posts, videos, and other educational resources.

Creating Attractive Course Landing Pages

Your course landing pages play a crucial role in converting visitors into customers. Here are some tips for creating compelling landing pages:

- Clear Call-to-Action: Include a clear and prominent call-to-action (CTA) that encourages visitors to take the desired action, whether it's purchasing the course or signing up for more information.

- Highlight Benefits: Clearly communicate the benefits and value of your courses, emphasizing how they can help solve your audience's problems or achieve their goals.

- Visual Appeal: Use high-quality images, videos, and graphics to make your landing pages visually appealing and engaging. A well-designed landing page can help capture the attention of visitors and keep them engaged.

Pricing Strategies for Different Markets

When pricing your courses, it's essential to consider factors such as market demand, competition, and perceived value. Here are some pricing strategies to consider:

- Tiered Pricing: Offer different pricing tiers with varying levels of access or additional benefits to appeal to different segments of your audience.

- Discounts and Promotions: Occasionally offer discounts or promotions to incentivize purchases and attract new customers.

- Bundle Deals: Bundle multiple courses together and offer them at a discounted price, providing added value for customers who purchase multiple courses.

In addition to the strategies discussed earlier in this chapter, there are several other important aspects to consider when marketing and selling your Master Resell Rights (MRR) courses. Let's explore these additional strategies to help you maximize your course sales and reach a wider audience.

Resale Strategies

When selling MRR courses, it's essential to consider different resale strategies to maximize your earning potential and cater to various buyer preferences.

- Exclusive Licensing: Offer exclusive licensing options to buyers who wish to purchase the rights to use the course content exclusively. Exclusive licensing agreements typically command higher prices and provide buyers with sole ownership of the course materials.

- Non-exclusive Licensing: Alternatively, offer non-exclusive licensing options that allow multiple buyers to purchase the course under non-exclusive terms. Non-exclusive licensing agreements are often more affordable and appeal to buyers looking for flexible usage rights.

- Bulk Sales to Educational Institutions: Explore opportunities to sell your courses in bulk to educational institutions, such as schools, colleges, and online learning platforms. Educational institutions often purchase courses in bulk to offer to their students or incorporate into their curriculum.

- Corporate Training Packages: Tailor your course content for corporate training programs and sell it to businesses looking to provide professional development opportunities for their employees. Corporate training packages can be customized to meet the specific needs and objectives of corporate clients.

Leveraging Affiliates and Partnerships

To increase the visibility and sales of your MRR courses, consider leveraging affiliates and building strategic partnerships with influencers and industry experts.

- Setting up an Affiliate Program: Create an affiliate program that allows individuals or businesses to promote your courses in exchange for a commission on sales. Affiliate marketing can help increase your course's reach and drive more sales through word-of-mouth referrals.

- Building Partnerships: Collaborate with influencers, bloggers, and industry experts in your niche to promote your courses to their audience. Building partnerships can help you tap into new markets and leverage the credibility and influence of trusted individuals within your industry.

Legal Considerations

Finally, it's essential to understand the legal considerations involved in selling MRR courses and ensure compliance with copyright and licensing laws.

- Understanding Copyright and Licensing Laws: Familiarize yourself with copyright laws and licensing agreements to ensure that you have the legal right to resell the course content. Avoid infringing on the intellectual property rights of others and ensure that you have the appropriate licenses to sell MRR courses.

- Drafting Clear Terms of Use and Privacy Policies: Clearly outline the terms of use and privacy policies governing the purchase and use of your courses. Provide transparent information to buyers regarding their rights and responsibilities, as well as how their personal data will be handled and protected.

With these valuable insights and strategies at your disposal, you're well-equipped to take your online course business to new heights. By implementing these marketing strategies and pricing tactics, you can effectively promote and sell your MRR courses, reaching a wider audience and maximizing your earning potential in the competitive online course market. In the final chapter of this guide, we'll wrap up our journey and leave you with some essential tips for long-term success. Let's finish strong!

Welcome to the final chapter of "From Purchase to Profit: A Beginner's Guide to Selling Online Courses." In this chapter, we'll explore strategies for scaling your sales and maximizing your earning potential in the online course market. As you continue to grow your business, it's essential to leverage feedback, explore new markets, and keep your courses relevant and up-to-date. Let's dive into some key tactics for scaling your sales effectively.

Using Feedback and Analytics to Refine Your Course and Marketing Approach

Feedback from your customers and analytics from your marketing efforts can provide valuable insights into areas for improvement and optimization. Here's how you can leverage feedback and analytics to refine your course and marketing approach:

- Customer Feedback: Encourage your customers to provide feedback on their learning experience, course content, and overall satisfaction. Use this feedback to identify strengths and weaknesses and make necessary improvements to your courses.

- Analytics Data: Analyze data from your website, email campaigns, and social media to gain insights into user behavior, engagement metrics, and conversion rates. Use this data to optimize your marketing strategies and improve the effectiveness of your sales funnels.

Exploring International Markets for Your Online Course

Expanding into international markets can open up new opportunities for growth and revenue. Here are some strategies for exploring international markets for your online course:

- Localization: Tailor your course content, marketing materials, and pricing to suit the preferences and cultural norms of your target international markets.

- Language Support: Offer your courses in multiple languages to appeal to a broader audience and make your content accessible to non-English speakers.

- Market Research: Conduct thorough market research to understand the needs, preferences, and buying behaviors of consumers in your target international markets.

Updating and Relaunching Your Course to Maintain Relevance and Interest

To keep your courses relevant and maintain ongoing interest from your audience, consider updating and relaunching your courses periodically. Here's how you can do it effectively:

- Content Updates: Stay informed about industry trends, developments, and changes, and update your course content accordingly to ensure it remains current and valuable to your audience.

- Relaunch Campaigns: Create buzz around your course updates and relaunches by implementing targeted marketing campaigns, offering special promotions, and leveraging social proof and testimonials.

- Continuous Improvement: Embrace a mindset of continuous improvement and strive to make incremental enhancements to your courses over time based on feedback and market trends.

By leveraging feedback, exploring international markets, and keeping your courses updated and relevant, you can effectively scale your sales and expand your reach in the competitive online course market. With dedication, persistence, and a willingness to adapt, you can achieve long-term success and profitability in your online course business.

Congratulations on completing "From Purchase to Profit: A Beginner's Guide to Selling Online Courses!" Armed with the knowledge and strategies shared in this guide, you're well-equipped to navigate the world of online course sales and build a thriving and profitable business. Best of luck on your journey to success!

Tips and Motivation

1. Stay Consistent: Building a successful online course business takes time and persistence. Stay consistent with your efforts, even when faced with challenges or setbacks. Rome wasn't built in a day, and neither is a thriving online business.

2. Embrace Continuous Learning: The world of online education is constantly evolving. Stay ahead of the curve by embracing continuous learning and staying updated on industry trends, technologies, and best practices.

3. Focus on Value: Your success in selling online courses hinges on the value you provide to your audience. Focus on creating high-quality, engaging content that addresses their needs and challenges. When you prioritize value, sales will naturally follow.

4. Build Relationships: Foster meaningful relationships with your audience by engaging with them regularly, responding to their feedback, and providing personalized support. Building trust and rapport with your customers is key to long-term success.

5. Celebrate Milestones: Take the time to celebrate your achievements, no matter how small. Whether it's hitting a sales milestone, receiving positive feedback from customers, or launching a new course, acknowledge and celebrate your progress along the way.

6. Stay Flexible: The online education landscape is dynamic and ever-changing. Stay flexible and open to new opportunities, trends, and strategies. Adapt and evolve your business model as needed to stay relevant and competitive in the market.

7. Don't Be Afraid to Fail: Failure is a natural part of the entrepreneurial journey. Don't be afraid to take risks, try new things, and learn from your mistakes. Every setback is an opportunity for growth and improvement.

8. Believe in Yourself: Above all, believe in yourself and your ability to succeed. Confidence and self-belief are powerful drivers of success. Trust in your vision, stay focused on your goals, and never underestimate the impact you can make in the world of online education.

Remember, success is not just about the destination, but the journey. Enjoy the process, stay passionate about your mission, and keep striving for greatness in everything you do. You've got this!

Conclusion

Congratulations on completing "From Purchase to Profit: A Beginner's Guide to Selling Online Courses!" Throughout this guide, we've explored the ins and outs of selling online courses and how you can leverage Master Resell Rights (MRR) and Private Label Rights (PLR) courses to build a profitable online education business.

Let's recap the importance and benefits of MRR and PLR courses:

- Time and Cost Efficiency: MRR and PLR courses allow you to bypass the time-consuming and costly process of creating courses from scratch, saving you valuable time and resources.

- Profit Potential: With MRR and PLR courses, you have the opportunity to generate passive income by reselling courses repeatedly without additional effort.

- Flexibility and Customization: While MRR courses offer ready-made content for resale, PLR courses provide the flexibility to modify, rebrand, and customize the content to suit your brand and audience's needs.

Building a sustainable online education business requires dedication, persistence, and a commitment to continuous improvement. Here are some final thoughts to help you on your journey:

- Focus on Quality: Prioritize quality in your courses and marketing efforts to attract and retain customers. Invest in creating valuable content that addresses the needs and interests of your target audience.

- Stay Relevant: Keep your courses up-to-date with industry trends and developments to maintain their relevance and appeal to your audience. Regularly update and refresh your course content to provide ongoing value to your customers.

- Engage Your Audience: Foster meaningful connections with your audience through engaging content, interactive experiences, and personalized communication. Listen to feedback, address concerns, and strive to exceed your customers' expectations.

In conclusion, selling online courses can be a rewarding and lucrative venture, especially when leveraging the power of MRR and PLR courses. By following the strategies and insights shared in this guide, you're well-equipped to embark on your journey to success in the online education industry. Remember, success doesn't happen overnight, but with dedication and perseverance, you can build a thriving online education business that generates passive income for years to come.

Thank you for joining us on this journey, and best of luck on your path to building a sustainable and profitable online course business!

Appendices

Glossary of Terms

- Master Resell Rights (MRR): A licensing agreement that allows individuals to resell a product and pass on the resell rights to their customers.

- Private Label Rights (PLR): A licensing agreement that allows individuals to modify, rebrand, and resell a product under their own brand name.

- Digital Products: Intangible goods that are delivered electronically, such as online courses, ebooks, software, and digital downloads.

- Affiliate Marketing: A marketing strategy where individuals promote products or services and earn a commission for each sale made through their referral.

- Copyright: Legal protection granted to the creators of original works, granting them exclusive rights to use and distribute their creations.

Additional Resources and Reading

- [Content Sparks](https://www.contentsparks.com/)

- [PLR.me](https://www.plr.me/)

- [Coach Glue](https://coachglue.com/)

- [Tools For Motivation](https://www.toolsformotivation.com/)

- [PLR Database](https://www.plrdatabase.net/)

- [Berkeley Wellbeing Institute](https://berkeleywellbeing.com/)

- [Problemio](https://www.problemio.com/)

- [PLR Products](https://www.plrproducts.com/)

FAQ about MRR and PLR Courses

Q: What is the difference between MRR and PLR courses?

A: MRR courses allow you to resell the product to others, while PLR courses grant you the flexibility to modify, rebrand, and resell the product under your own brand name.

Q: Can I customize MRR courses?

A: No, MRR courses typically come as ready-made products that cannot be modified or rebranded. However, you can still resell them to others.

Q: Are there any legal implications when selling MRR and PLR courses?

A: Yes, it's essential to understand and comply with copyright and licensing laws when selling MRR and PLR courses. Always ensure that you have the appropriate rights to resell the products and adhere to any terms and conditions outlined in the licensing agreement.

Q: How can I market MRR and PLR courses effectively?

A: Effective marketing strategies for MRR and PLR courses include leveraging social media, email marketing, SEO, creating attractive course landing pages, and setting up affiliate programs.

Q: Are there any restrictions on who can purchase MRR and PLR courses?

A: While there are typically no restrictions on who can purchase MRR and PLR courses, it's essential to review the terms and conditions of each product to ensure compliance with any licensing agreements.

Q: Can I offer refunds for MRR and PLR courses?

A: Refund policies for MRR and PLR courses may vary depending on the seller's terms and conditions. It's advisable to have a clear refund policy in place and communicate it to your customers before making a purchase.

Q: How do I handle customer support for MRR and PLR courses?

A: Providing excellent customer support is essential for building trust and credibility with your customers. Be responsive to inquiries, address any issues or concerns promptly, and strive to provide value-added support to enhance the customer experience.

References

1. Content Sparks. (n.d.). Retrieved from https://www.contentsparks.com/

2. PLR.me. (n.d.). Retrieved from https://www.plr.me/

3. Coach Glue. (n.d.). Retrieved from https://coachglue.com/

4. Tools For Motivation. (n.d.). Retrieved from https://www.toolsformotivation.com/

5. PLR Database. (n.d.). Retrieved from https://www.plrdatabase.net/

6. Berkeley Wellbeing Institute. (n.d.). Retrieved from https://berkeleywellbeing.com/

7. Problemio. (n.d.). Retrieved from https://www.problemio.com/

8. PLR Products. (n.d.). Retrieved from https://www.plrproducts.com/

Further Reading

- Smith, J. (2023). *The Ultimate Guide to Online Course Creation.* Publisher.

- Johnson, K. (2022). *Master Resell Rights Mastery: How to Maximize Profits with MRR Courses.* Publisher.

- White, A. (2021). *Private Label Profits: The Insider's Guide to PLR Success.* Publisher.